Introduction

CW01668906

Eureka! is a topic-based series from **Channel 4 Schools** intended as a resource for teachers of 7 – 11 year olds. Across the academic year, the series offers separate units which relate to many of the National Curriculum topics in England, Wales and Northern Ireland and the environmental studies themes in Scotland. The focus of each unit emphasises a principal subject but the content within the programmes relates to other key areas of the curriculum.

History Through Art is a unit of programmes which uses art to present six different periods in history. 'Every picture tells a story' is the theme of this unit and six pieces of art, one per programme, are featured with each one revealing fascinating insights into life in times past.

Works of art are not simply evidence of how things looked at a particular time, they represent the point of view of the artist. In order to look in detail at these pieces and question their portrayal of events, each of the programmes draws on a key character from the period to tell the story from their point of view.

The story narratives arising from the pictures illustrate the power of art as evidence in history and its ability to generate curiosity and raise questions about content.

Channel 4 is always keen to receive comments about both the programmes and the Teachers' Guides. Please send any correspondence to:

Adrienne Jones
Education Officer
Channel 4 Schools
PO Box 100
Warwick
CV34 6TZ

It is highly recommended that you obtain posters of all three pictures (for availability see insert).

History Through Art and the curriculum

The excitement of the world of art is presented in these six programmes. There is the skill of the painter and craft of the embroiderer to be enjoyed, but also much more.

The pictures which have been selected are ones which are firmly linked with six popular areas of study within history:

Programme 1 – **The Tomb of Nebamun:** The Ancient Egyptians

Programme 2 – **Paintings on Pots:** The Ancient Greeks

Programme 3 – **Pictures from Pompeii:** The Romans

Programme 4 – **The Bayeux Tapestry:** Saxons and Normans

Programme 5 – **Sir Henry Unton:** The Tudors

Programme 6 – **The Railway Station:** The Victorians

All these works of art focus on aspects of everyday life. From the interior of a pyramid, a wall painting thousands of years old depicts the afterlife of Nebamun the scribe. The intricate detail of pictures painted using clay slip on the pots of Ancient Greece, show a remarkable range of fact and fantasy. The sophisticated portrait of the Roman couple from Pompeii reflects their upwardly mobile lifestyle.

The programmes all involve people in some way but not every picture offers a personal life history – whilst the painting of Sir Henry Unton with its biographical narrative and symbolism uses colour and light for effect, the textile art of the Bayeux Tapestry is presented in a linear, almost 'comic-strip' format and The Railway Station with its panorama of the station interior, could almost be extended as a wall frieze.

Amidst these works of art, there exists an intriguing weave of subject matter which integrates in a cross-curricular way with geography, science and maths, stories, poems, dance and music. The content of the programmes could be equally linked with topics on Transport, Clothes, Colour, Other countries.

The Teachers' Guide

The programmes give rise to a range of activities which focus primarily on understanding history but also on ways of helping children develop skills to 'read' pictures together with a confidence about looking at them and using them.

The suggested activities encourage the children to guess, surmise, deduct and hypothesise as they share their ideas and gradually 'unpack' each picture. Also within the activities are drama and role-play suggestions to encourage empathy with the people in the pictures as well as questions to encourage prediction skills and the imagination.

Artwork is one of many sources of historical evidence and the use of pictures as a primary source of material can present some problems. For instance, a work of art can give a fairly accurate representation of the way people and places looked, but the 'truth' of the scene will depend entirely on the effect the artist wanted to create. Rarely would the artist be concerned just with producing an accurate documentary record and the children need to become aware of this.

How to look at a painting

As 'picture detectives' the children will need to be able to ask questions of the picture.

The children could use a viewfinder and magnifying glasses to select a part of the picture to home in on. These will be a great help in looking at small detail.

The pictures

- Who painted it? When? Where? Why? How?
- Who was it painted for?
- What are the different materials used?
- How has light and shade been used in the picture?
- Compare the skills of the artists.
- Compare the pictures.
- Which picture do you like, and why?
- What might have been left out? Why?

Costume

- What are the favourite colours for clothes?
- Identify the work clothes.
- Identify simple types of fabric.
- Identify styles of make-up.
- Imagine what the clothes feel like to wear.

Other aspects

- What do the facial expressions convey; is it sensible to judge character by facial expression?
- What does the composition of the group say? For example, find the most important person in the group.
- Who are the different people in the painting and what are their jobs?
- How can the important people be identified?
- Does it show us what people really looked like? How do you know?
- Does the painting tell us anything about the roles of men and women in society?
- What clues does the background give about the way of life? Is the background a real scene (indoor or outdoor) or is it not in the real space at all?
- Was the artist really there when the scene took place?
- Does the painting show life as it really was?

Children can also be encouraged to approach the work through the senses, imagining what it might be like to actually be present.

- What kinds of sounds might be heard?
- What kinds of smells might there be?
- What about any objects in the picture, how might they feel?

PROGRAMMES	CONTENT	CROSS-CURRICULAR
❶ **The Tomb of Nebamun**	• Egyptian artists' tools, materials and techniques • lifestyle of an Egyptian nobleman • beliefs about the afterlife • background information on farming/agriculture • symbolism in Egyptian painting	**History:** factual knowledge and understanding of Ancient Egyptian lifestyle: skills in using historical sources to find evidence **Geography:** the farming year **English:** speaking and listening, descriptive writing **Art:** developing critical skills, experimenting with different perspectives **Drama:** role-play
❷ **Paintings on Pots**	• Greek potters' tools, materials and techniques • ancient Greece, its lifestyle, beliefs, mythology etc, seen through pottery decoration • historical events – background information • role of pottery as a primary historical source	**History:** factual understanding and knowledge of Ancient Greek lifestyle and systems: skills in using historical sources to find evidence **English:** speaking and listening, asking questions about the past, creative writing, vocabulary **Drama:** mime, mask and chorus **Art:** designing, painting and clay work **Philosophy:** learning to debate an issue
❸ **Pictures from Pompeii**	• painting and mosaic of the period: technique, subject, purpose • lifestyle of Pompeii, AD 79, reflected through a portrait • role of the archaeologist in interpreting a major historical event	**History:** factual knowledge of lifestyle in Pompeii; of the role of painting and mosaic; of the natural disaster of AD 79: skills in using historical sources to find evidence **English:** speaking and listening, asking questions about the past; creative and descriptive writing **Research skills:** learning to conduct research effectively at a basic level **Drama:** role-play **Art:** painting/mosaic/sculpture
❹ **The Bayeux Tapestry**	• museum, map, the Bayeux Tapestry • Walter de Caen – Norman soldier • tapestry replica being sewn • Saxon women's view of events	**History:** the story of the tapestry, Saxons and Normans **Geography:** mapwork **English:** drama, role-play **D & T:** brochure making (I.T.), designing artefacts, textiles **Art:** illustrative skills, colour studies, materials and media selections **English:** descriptive writing, story-telling, animation, sequencing **Maths:** distance and measurement
❺ **Sir Henry Unton**	• class topic – Tudors, oil painting, Sir Henry Unton's life • life in a Tudor country mansion music, dance	**History:** the life and times of Sir Henry Unton, a Tudor ambassador **Geography:** tracing Unton's travels **English:** general oracy **Art:** appreciation, Tudor mini-portraits **Dance and music:** of the Tudor period **D & T:** designing clothing
❺ **The Railway Station**	• modern-day Paddington station • lifestyle of Victorian people • costume, travel	**History:** travel and dress in Victorian times **English:** story-telling, writing **Drama:** role-play **Geography:** rail routes **Art:** colour matching **Music:** environmental sounds

PROGRAMME

1 The Tomb of Nebamun

Programme outline

This programme features the beautiful wall paintings recovered from the tomb of Nebamun, the scribe, and now housed in the British Museum. They show scenes of everyday life in Egypt as it was 3,500 years ago and constitute an exciting primary source, rich in detailed visual information.

Menna, the tomb painter, 'comes to life' to describe the materials used to create the paintings, to explain the context in which they were produced and to guide the children to look closely at particularly interesting fragments which provide a fascinating insight into the way of life of a man of relatively high status in Ancient Egypt.

The children will see Nebamun (an official in the 18th dynasty, 1500 BC) hunting in the marshes with his wife, Hatshepsut, and his daughter; at a feast where he is entertained by dancers and musicians, as well as various agricultural scenes – all of which, together, yield a wealth of visual evidence – birds, fish and other animals, trees, crops, plants, clothes and hairstyles, tools, food, furniture, etc – from which the children will learn much about Ancient Egypt. The children are encouraged to look closely, to question and interpret, and to consider the symbolism of the paintings.

NB This series of paintings is currently undergoing restoration and will not be on view to the public for approximately five years (see insert).

Key features

- Historical enquiry
- Everyday life in ancient Egypt
- Materials, tools and techniques in Egyptian art
- Symbolism

Before viewing

▶ Explain to the children that they are about to see paintings recovered from the tomb of Nebamun, whose precise job was that of grain accountant, and who lived in Egypt 3,500 years ago. The fact that his tomb was elaborately painted is an indication of the status of his job in Ancient Egyptian times. You may wish to point out that the scenes represent the good things in Nebamun's life, which he would once again enjoy in his afterlife. Tell the class the story behind the paintings on page 6.

Whilst viewing

▶ Encourage the children to look very closely at the detail within each painting and to think about what this tells us about life in Ancient Egypt. You may wish to pause the video at various points in the programme.

After viewing

About the paintings

▶ Ask the children to see just how much they can find out about Nebamun and his lifestyle by studying reproductions of the tomb paintings and answering the following (by no means comprehensive) list of questions. The beauty of this activity is that it does not require highly developed reading skills, yet it encourages careful observation and historical enquiry.

- Can children identify the different birds, fish and other animals?
- What does the painting tells us about clothing, hairstyles, jewellery, farming, hunting methods, trees and plants, entertainment, work?
- Are there any clues to indicate what might be in the missing parts? (The end of a spear can be seen in the bottom left-hand corner of 'Fowling in the Marshes' and is all that remains of the other half of this painting, which is now lost, but which was photographed long ago and which, experts say, showed Nebamun spearing fish.)

Art activities

▶ Encourage children to make aesthetic judgements about the paintings – do they like the colours, style, use of perspective? Can they explain why?

▶ Ask the children to draw each other from different perspectives, using strong lines to define shapes. They could then produce a painting in which two or more views are combined. Encourage them to think carefully about the colours they will use and to outline the main shapes boldly.

▶ Younger children may wish to paint a garden scene, Egyptian style, in which trees, plants and flowers are 'flattened out' and laid out in rows or grids. Provide a variety of plants and/or flowers as a stimulus, in order to avoid formless or repetitive representations.

▶ Give the children a photocopy of 'Fowling in the Marshes' (see insert) with space at the side, and ask them to draw the rest of the scene as they imagine it.

A day in the life of ...

▶ The children should have enough information about Nebamun and his lifestyle to be able to write a diary-style description of a day in his life. Encourage the children to look again at the paintings, if necessary, and to imagine the sounds, smells, tastes, weather, etc.

Wanted – tomb painter

▶ Ask the children to imagine that they are applying for a job as a tomb painter for Nebamun. Encourage them to think about and list all the skills and experience they can offer. For example, being able to provide their own brushes and paints, a steady hand, attention to detail, ability to use their imagination (paint Nebamun as he would like to be remembered, not as he actually is).

Invitation to a feast

▶ Ask the children to design an invitation to a feast to be held to celebrate Nebamun's birthday. They should specify what clothes and jewellery are to be worn by the guests and should give details of where the party will be held (in Nebamun's garden?), what food, music and other entertainment will be provided. Less able children could use the Activity sheet provided on page 7.

Farming

▶ Ask the children to find out about farming in Ancient Egypt and, in particular, the dependence of farmers on the River Nile and its regular flooding pattern. The children could draw or paint a frieze showing the different activities carried out during the year. More able children could present this as a pie chart.

Interview with Nebamun

▶ In pairs, the children could enact an interview with Nebamun, asking him questions about his life, work and family, leisure activities, etc, as well as about his journey to the afterlife. What happened at the weighing of the heart ceremony? What shabti figures did he choose to have placed in his tomb? etc. This could be recorded on cassette, perhaps as part of a series of interviews with people from history.

The Tomb of Nebamun

background information

The story behind the paintings

Almost everything we know about Ancient Egypt comes from the paintings, papyri and artefacts found in tombs, as well as from the tombs themselves. Unfortunately, many tombs have been looted, their contents stolen and the paintings lost or damaged in the process. In some cases, however, paintings have been recovered and thus saved for posterity. The eleven paintings from Nebamun's tomb, now held at the British Museum in London, are some of the most beautiful ever found.

Nebamun lived, worked and was buried in Thebes, on the eastern side of the River Nile, approximately 3,500 years ago. He worked for the king and, in his capacity as grain accountant, was responsible for the food supplied for the citizens of Thebes. Because the art of hieroglyphic writing was complex and difficult to learn, few people in ancient Egypt were able to read and write, but Nebamun was one of these few and, as a scribe, enjoyed some status in Egyptian society. Only important people were able to afford to have a tomb built and decorated with elaborate paintings and Nebamun, who was in this privileged position, commissioned the construction of his tomb before he died. Workmen used stone hammers and bronze chisels to dig into the hillside, carving rooms and passageways out of the rock. The walls were covered with a rough plaster, made from mud and straw, and this in turn was covered with a fine, smooth plaster to give a suitable surface on which to paint.

Painting facts

Working by lamplight, artists began to work as soon as the plaster was dry, firstly marking out a grid on the walls by applying string dipped in red paint. This grid ensured the even size and proportions of the figures, their correct alignment and accurate spacing. Outlines were drawn first and subsequently colour was applied using pigments made by crushing chalk, stone and minerals found in the desert. Finally, another outline was added to give definition. Artists took care to represent their subject favourably, i.e. as they wanted to appear, rather than as they were. Hence Nebamun is depicted as a young man, slim and handsome, although experts believe he was probably quite old when the pictures were painted. Reeds, which had been softened by chewing, were used to apply the paint and the rich variety of textural detail in Nebamun's tomb painting shows the artists' skill and expertise in creating a variety of surfaces to represent fur, feathers, scales and fabric. Above the figures, and in any blank spaces, hieroglyphs were added to enhance and explain each image. Those beside Nebamun in the 'Fowling in the Marshes' painting, for example, refer to his enjoyment of seeing the good things.

Perspective was interesting. With human figures faces appear in profile and eyes appear front on. The torso usually appears front on, too, but arms and legs appear in profile.

In representations of gardens, trees and plants are shown, as on a map, but 'flattened out', as in the painting 'Garden with fish pond', where the long sides are arranged in registers with the trees at the back painted above, and those in front painted below the pond.

The various components in the banquet painting are separated by black lines, each part showing different elements of the same scene. The fish at the bottom of the painting is a talapia. The female protects her young by holding them in her mouth and spitting them out when danger is past. This action is thought to symbolise reincarnation.

It is 200 years since Nebamun's tomb in Thebes was last seen, since it has now been either destroyed or covered by sand and stone and its exact location is no longer known. It is known that the eleven paintings held at the British Museum constitute only a part of the whole painting, or series of paintings.

YOU ARE INVITED TO A PARTY TO BE HELD IN

TO MARK THE OCCASION OF NEBAMUN'S BIRTHDAY.

YOU WILL BE ENTERTAINED BY

FOOD WILL INCLUDE

PLEASE WEAR

2 Paintings on Pots

Programme outline

In this programme we visit the Ashmolean Museum in Oxford, and the British Museum in London. Both are home to fine examples of Greek pottery – one of the historian's richest sources of information about Ancient Greek civilisation, particularly since 500 BC.

We meet a potter, Nikias, who demonstrates the properties of clay and shows how he makes pots. Then the painter's craft is considered using a clay slip which looks invisible when painted on, he creates the classical styles of design and the practical method of achieving the finished result – black on red or red on black.

The range of subject matter for these designs is vast, covering every aspect of everyday life in Greece and reporting on major events such as the games at Olympia and famous battles at sea and on land. Nor did the painter confine himself to realism but frequently depicted his own version of traditional religious belief and mythology, telling of the particular exploits and attributes of the many gods and the challenges faced by such heroes as Herakles, Jason and Odysseus.

According to size and shape, pots were created for a specific purpose reflected in the subject of the painting. So the lekythos, a pot traditionally used at funerals, might be decorated with scenes of mourning and burial processions of the past based on reality or mythology. No subject would be considered too trivial or too sacred to be addressed.

Key features

- Archaeology – primary sources of evidence
- Evidence through craft – pottery
- Lifestyle, historical events, religion and mythology in Ancient Greece

Before viewing

▶ Identify modern Greece on a map and ask the children what they know about the country. Encourage them to bring any artefacts to share with the class.

▶ Establish whether or not the children have any knowledge of the history of Greece and the time scale involved. Point out the position of Crete, Athens, Sparta and Macedonia on a map and explain that the names, areas and government of Greek territory have altered many times in the thousands of years of their civilisation.

Whilst viewing

▶ Ask the children to observe how pots were made and decorated. Why use clay? Why are pots of such importance to archaeologists and historians?

▶ Ask them to consider what other artefacts might be available to archaeologists investigating the history of early Greece. What artefacts are less available and why?

After viewing

About Greek pots

▶ Ensure that there is plenty of visual material available to the children while these points are discussed:

- What do historians know about the manufacture of Greek pottery? Were pots made in one piece?
- What subjects can be seen depicted on pots? What shapes, sizes, functions of pots have the children observed? Why have such a wide range? What advantage is there in storing wine, oil, perfume in pots made of clay?
- How did the potters achieve the red and black colours? Why not employ other colours? How was the paint put on? Share the information on page 10 with the class.

The pot painter's art

▶ Discuss important events in our recent history, for example the Labour party coming to power. Imagining themselves to be pot painters, the children should create a design reflecting the chosen event using red and black paper or black and red paint.

▶ Children should be given the experience of handling and working with clay, making thumb pots and trying out the coil technique used to make larger pots. If the school has access to a kiln these could be fired, glazed and re-fired, comparing our colouring techniques with those of the Greek potter. A display of pots, old and new, would demonstrate how design changes occur more frequently in modern times.

Myths

▶ Ask the children to recall the myths mentioned in the programme. Discuss other myths known to the children and read various examples to them. What elements do these stories often have in common? Consider the theme of challenge, the test of personal courage, punishment for angering the gods, quests to win over new territory, etc.

▶ Ask the children to create a monster comparing examples such as the Minotaur, Cyclops, Medusa, etc. Consider what challenge or trap this monster might devise to protect itself and write a class story in which a man or woman is sent to destroy it. What will the reward be for succeeding? How might they defy the creature? Children could work individually or in pairs, planning the myth in note form before they write. The story could be presented with a design for a pot and a large illustration of the monster, giving less able children a chance to work in a productive team where they have a clear role.

Pot shapes

▶ Working in groups, children could be given the 'shards' of several broken utensils, saucers, plates, etc. Their task would be to number each piece and reform the original using PVA glue, working as an organised team of archaeologists. Better still if these could be 'found' buried in sand or earth. The safety element would need to be emphasised and protective gloves worn.

▶ Children should investigate the types of pot traditionally used by the Greeks. Using Activity sheet 2, they should label each one with its Greek name, giving its purpose and most likely contents. Children might also consider an appropriate subject for decorating each type of pot.

▶ Obviously, the history of the Greeks is a major topic. If time and curriculum demands allow, mini-topic research areas might include:

sport in the life of ancient Greeks
gods and goddesses
Greek architecture
the battle of Thermopylai
life of a boy in Sparta
role of women and girls
clothing
homes
food and drink
theatre

This could be prescribed research in which teachers prepare in advance questions to be investigated in the chosen area. This approach helps children to home in on the most relevant areas and can be tailored to ability. A time limit might be useful.

Words and meanings

▶ Children may enjoy comparison of the Greek alphabet with our own. A list of words commonly used in English and derived from the Greek could be offered to more able children who should seek dictionary definitions in a timed exercise. Discussions about the wealth of sources in language – borrowed words etc, would be appropriate here. An obvious starting point is the word 'alphabet'.

Mask mime

▶ Using traditional myths with the option of making masks to convey role as in the Greek theatre, children could devise mime which recreates their chosen story. Groups could decide to use a Greek 'chorus' to narrate the events of the mime.

What do you think?

▶ Explain that the term 'philosophy' is about the pursuit of wisdom and discuss how Ancient Greeks such as Socrates and Plato taught and learnt through asking questions and debate. Show the children that they too can be philosophers simply by thinking about questions such as 'Is it right to kill?' 'What happens when we die?' 'Should you be nice to other people and if so, why?'

Paintings on Pots

background information

The story behind the evidence

Greek history dates from approximately 2000 BC when Minoan civilisation was at its height on the island of Crete. Since that time history tells us of the development of Athens and Sparta, the strife between city states, kingdoms and democracies, wars at sea and on land, the expansion and contraction of territories under Greek domination, all taking place on a rich background of everyday life. But how do we know?

Fortunately, many sources of information have been passed down in written form. There is less evidence through paintings since most have been destroyed. Copies do remain from later periods but are less reliable. Evidence of architecture is abundant but gives us information of a very specific nature. Archaeologists and historians have therefore relied on pottery to extend and confirm visually knowledge gleaned from the written word.

The tradition of decorating pots extends to the present day. The subject matter depicted and the changes in black/red, red/black design techniques, mean that any given pot found in an archaeological dig can be dated with some accuracy. Greek pots and the stories and information represented in their decoration have been, and remain, a vibrant record of the lifestyle of this people, a primary source of evidence through art.

Wherever the Greeks settled they took the craft of the potter and the painter with them and since pots were often entombed with their owners many have been preserved intact. The pots speak to us of every aspect of life from the most basic to the most influential and spiritual: scenes of a child being potty trained; graphic episodes of battles; athletes taking part in the games at Olympia; simple family burial rites; traditional stories from mythology or featuring the many gods and representing their particular area of influence; actors preparing for performances in the theatre; musicians practising on the lyre.

Pot painting facts

All are presented in the simple form of black images on the red clay, or later, the red clay of the images exposed in a black surround. After the pot has been thrown it is painted with a diluted clay mixture called slip. When applied, the slip shows up as the same colour as the red clay. It is not until it is put in the kiln, that the slip turns black and the rest of the pot red. The red colour was the product of a clay rich in iron which produced its colour during the firing process.

Small details on red figures were painted on using a fine brush, a bristle, or a fine nozzle: on black figures details were cut into the clay with a sharp point. Most pots were turned on a wheel operated either by hand or foot. Very large pots were made by hand using the coil technique. Handles were attached using slip.

There were three styles of pottery. The first consisted of black figures on a red background. Around 530 BC the trend was to reverse the red and black like a negative.

Spot the pot!

Name: ____________________

Use: ____________________

Name: ____________________

Use: ____________________

Name: ____________________

Use: ____________________

Name: ____________________

Use: ____________________

Name: ____________________

Use: ____________________

Name: ____________________

Use: ____________________

▶ How many more shapes of pot can you find in your research?

PROGRAMME

3 Pictures from Pompeii

Programme outline

At the British Museum, the cold, formal visual impact of Roman statues is contrasted with the colourful realism of paintings from a similar period. The programme then focuses on a wall painting found in the ruins of Pompeii which features Terentius Neo, a baker, painted with his wife. For the purpose of the programme his wife has been named Julia. It is she who describes life in Pompeii at the time of the eruption of Vesuvius in AD 79. She then speaks of her own life as a baker's wife.

Julia's role is to keep the accounts while her husband runs the practical side of the bakery: the business is successful and they live well. We see them sitting for the portrait, dressed fashionably, with Terentius holding the business deeds and Julia the stylus and writing tablet used in her work.

They have also commissioned a sketch of their dog, Argus, which will form the basic design for a mosaic. The methods of painting and making mosaics are compared. At this point the first effects of the eruption are witnessed, building up to a climax in which Terentius, Julia and Argus are seen dying. The final scenes of the programme take us to the eighteenth century when archaeologists first began seriously to excavate the site of Pompeii. Out of the remains are unearthed paintings and mosaics including the examples described in the programme.

Key features

- Evidence through art
- Lifestyle in a Roman community
- Impact of major historical event
- Role of archaeology in primary sources

Before viewing

▶ Identify modern Italy on a map and ask the children what they know of the country.

▶ Establish whether or not the children have any knowledge of the history of Pompeii. Point out its position on a map and discuss why this site might have been chosen for a town. What advantages or disadvantages might there be in building a town close to Mount Vesuvius?

Whilst viewing

▶ What information do we gain about Terentius and Julia from the instructions given to the artist?

▶ What do we learn about the different techniques used in painting and mosaic work?

After viewing

About the painting and mosaic

- What does the painting tell us about Terentius and Julia? What evidence is there to tell us that they run a successful business?
- Why do the children think the couple have chosen to be painted looking straight at the viewer? What messages might they be trying to give?
- What do Julia's hairstyle and clothes suggest about her? What items are the couple holding? Do the portrait and Julia's comments allow us to draw any conclusions about the role of women in Pompeian society?
- What might the advantages be in having a portrait painted rather than relying on present day techniques such as photography, videos and television?
- Where would mosaics and paintings be found in Pompeii? On the mosaic of Argus appear the words 'cave canem' (beware of the dog). Ask the children what this means and why might Julia and Terentius have commissioned the artist to make the mosaic?
- Why do you think paintings and mosaics might have survived so well in the ruins?

The history of Pompeii

▶ Discuss what has been learnt about life in Pompeii in AD 79. It may be an appropriate point to give the class further information using page 14 as a starting point.

▶ Discuss the different sources of information available to historians studying the history of Pompeii. How does this compare with sources of evidence relating to prehistoric times?

▶ Life in Pompeii offers a wealth of fascinating mini-topic areas for children to investigate. To ensure that research is of value it is advisable for children to define clearly in advance what they hope to discover, possibly by drawing up a set number of questions for investigation which relate appropriately to individual ability. Topic areas might include:

design and role of public baths
housing
gods and goddesses
theatre
gladiatorial activities
food preparation and diet
clothing
household artefacts
farming/winemaking
painting and mosaic
four styles in Pompeian painting
bakeries
dyeing and fulling
the eruption of Vesuvius, AD 79

▶ Using the house plan offered as Activity sheet 3, page 15, children should list five twentieth-century items in each room which they consider would make interesting artefacts for archaeologists to unearth in the thirty-eighth century assuming that Britain were subject to a similar eruption in the near future.

Name that object

▶ Children could be asked to describe to others one of their chosen artefacts from the preceding activity without naming it. How quickly can the audience identify the item?

A letter home

▶ Discuss the role of freedmen and slaves in Pompeian society. An employee of Terentius' at the bakery and a domestic servant, undoubtedly slaves, are featured in the programme. Children capable of personal investigative work could be encouraged to research either home life or the work of a baker in first-century Pompeii. Speaking as a slave they could then write a letter to a family member about working conditions, life in Pompeii, etc.

Role play

▶ Discuss with the children the advantages of having a portrait painted, e.g. features can be subtly altered to suit the whims of the sitter. Ask children to share what they consider to be their best and/or worst features. How would they like to be painted? Full face? In profile? Sewing? Holding a fishing rod?

Now, working in pairs with one person taking the role of the artist, the sitter should discuss with the artist how they would like to be presented in a portrait. After a fixed time the roles should be reversed.

Mosaic matters

▶ Simple artefacts, for example bowls of flowers, jugs, a stool, a hat, could serve as a stimulus for bold outline drawings. A mosaic could then be torn or cut from paper or card painted in the required colours or by choosing appropriate coloured pieces from magazines. Depending on the size of the work this could be done individually or in groups. Enlargement of the original drawing would introduce children to practical use of grids of different sizes.

The portrait of Terentius Neo and Julia, his wife

background information

The story behind the painting

Pompeii was originally chosen as the site for a town because of its situation near the sea, which was crucial for trading, and its position near the slopes of Vesuvius, which were ideally placed for farming and the cultivation of vineyards. As the town developed, its streets were built on a grid system, each section enclosing a jigsaw of shops, taverns, housing, public baths, temples, shrines, theatres, an amphitheatre, the main forum where all important commercial, religious, political and legal affairs were conducted, sports grounds, tombs, and small business outlets, including dyers and fullers, winemakers and bakers. Slaves and freedmen, rich and poor, lived side by side.

For years Vesuvius had lain dormant but in AD 62 a violent earthquake occurred, damaging many buildings and serving as a serious warning of what was to come in the future. Restoration of damaged buildings was in progress but not completed when the final devastating eruption occurred on 24 August AD 79. There was little warning and thousands of inhabitants were buried under the ash, lava and pumice. Most who had escaped from the city also died, overcome by the asphyxiating sulphur fumes and gases. Within a few hours a thriving community was silenced. No serious archaeology was undertaken until the eighteenth century in spite of random finds, pillaging and amateurish digs over the preceding centuries. As the importance of the ruins was recognised, sophisticated techniques were gradually introduced to ensure that artefacts and human and animal remains were sited and recorded accurately.

Fiorelli discovered that ash and pumice mixed with water had gradually hardened, enclosing human and animal remains. As flesh and clothing had dematerialised so the remaining skeletons remained in cavities. It was discovered that if plaster was pumped into such a cavity a 3D cast of the body was created bearing the marks of clothing, shoes, etc transferred from the imprints retained in the surrounding matter.

It was also established that four styles of wall painting had evolved during the development of Pompeii, often depicting architectural features which embellished otherwise plain accommodation, since furniture – made in stone, wood or tufa – was usually kept to a minimum. Mosaics were abundant.
The painting featured in this programme would have been situated on the front wall of the bakery. Julia is holding a stylus and writing tablet. A thin layer of wax would be spread onto the tablet and accounts written onto it with the stylus.

Picture facts

Like many wives of freedmen or citizens Julia would have a specific and important role in the business. Terentius holds the deeds of the business. Their direct look, full face, may have been chosen to suggest candour and integrity. Fashionable clothes and hairstyles would also reflect status and a successful lifestyle. Mosaics such as that of Argus would no doubt have formed part of the floor at the entrance to a house or shop. The couple would have lived in a typical house with a central atrium around which would be built bedrooms, a dining room, a small kitchen and toilet. Most houses had gardens.

Artefacts of the future

Bathroom

1. ______
2. ______
3. ______
4. ______
5. ______

Bedroom

1. ______
2. ______
3. ______
4. ______
5. ______

Playroom

1. ______
2. ______
3. ______
4. ______
5. ______

Kitchen

1. ______
2. ______
3. ______
4. ______
5. ______

Sitting Room

1. ______
2. ______
3. ______
4. ______
5. ______

Dining Room

1. ______
2. ______
3. ______
4. ______
5. ______

Garage

1. ______
2. ______
3. ______
4. ______
5. ______

The Bayeux Tapestry

Programme outline

The venue for this programme is the Museum of Reading which houses an exact replica of the Bayeux Tapestry. Fights and feastings, boats and battles, archers and horses – this tapestry has it all but it needs searching for and that's just what a class of children are intent on doing.

Before looking in detail at the tapestry, the children look at a map highlighting the route the Norman invaders took. A closer look at the tapestry itself reveals details of Norman and Saxon lifestyle. Cooking utensils, drinking cups and food are illustrated alongside farming and hunting scenes, boats and buildings.

Walter of Caen, a Norman character in the tapestry, 'comes alive' to tell the children his version of the events leading to the battle. Meanwhile, in the dimly-lit room of a Saxon castle, the scene of women seated around a table sewing the tapestry is interrupted by the granddaughter of one of them who plies her grandmother with questions about the tapestry – from a Saxon point of view.

Key features

- Communication through narrative structure
- Invasion and settlement
- Reasons for historical event
- Lifestyle

Before viewing

▶ Stress to the class that although the people might look a little cartoon-like they were real people and when not involved with fighting, they would have been farmers, masons, beekeepers, rich or poor, beggars and thieves, potters, builders and fishermen, fowlers, hunters, weavers and carvers.

▶ Tell the children the story depicted by the tapestry (see page 18).

Whilst viewing

Encourage the class to look closely at the detail within the tapestry and the method used for sewing it by pausing at these points in the programme.

After viewing

About the picture

▶ Only about one-third of the picture is about the Battle of Hastings. There is a whole lot more to the tapestry than the invasion and subsequent battle. Ask the class to recall what they can about the different aspects within the programme.

The Bayeux Tapestry comic strip

▶ On Activity sheet 4 are a number of scenes from the Bayeux Tapestry. The children are asked to write a caption under each one. The activity could be extended by listing the detail in the drawings and adding comments about these.

A Saxon tale (using the poster)

▶ Either in pairs or a small group the children select a Saxon in the tapestry who fits one of these descriptions:

Grumpy	Boastful	Cheery
Brave	Forgetful	Homesick

They then pretend that they are that person and tell a partner:

- Who they are and what they did before the battle.
- What happened to them at the Battle of Hastings.

The children could extend this activity by writing one week of a diary during a particularly interesting part of the adventure.

Puppets

▶ In groups of three or four, the children could make puppets based on characters from the tapestry. The figures could be copied onto card, cut out and stuck on a thin roll of newspaper. Pieces of fabric for clothes and string for hair could be added.

Once made, the puppets can be used to enact a short scene from the tapestry.

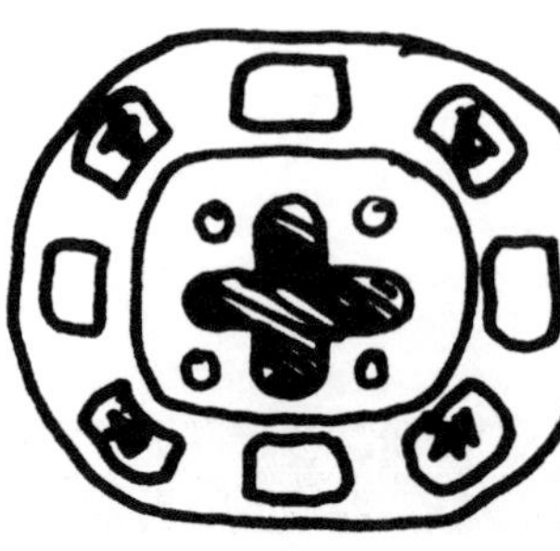

Make a piece of Saxon or Norman jewellery

▶ Saxons made wonderful jewellery. Poorer people wore cross-shaped bronze brooches. Rich people wore circular clasps in gold and silver.

- The children will need a piece of clay about the size of a golf ball (they could also use salt-dough), which is pinched into shape to make a thickish Saxon clasp or cross.
- The next task is to either make a box or find one it will fit into and line it with fabric and padding to make it look extremely precious.
- The children can then decorate the box outside by sticking small, light items such as snipped-up milk straws, twigs, small stones onto it. Once they have stuck firmly, the boxes can be sprayed silver, gold or bronze.
- A piece of paper can be fitted inside the lid of the box explaining who owned the jewel.

Tapestry tour

▶ Using atlases, the children could plan a Bayeux Tapestry Tour that begins in their home town. It will be a circular coach tour visiting these places:

Stamford Bridge (near York)

Pevensey (where William landed)

Hastings (where the battle was fought)

Waltham Abbey (William's tomb)

Westminster Church (where Harold was crowned)

▶ They could make an illustrated brochure to capture people's attention. The brochure needs an attractive front cover. The contents could include:

- A very clear map of the road routes
- The mileage between each place
- The time it will take to get to each place
- The towns which will be used as overnight stops
- The length of the tour
- The cost per person

▶ Each page could have suitable illustrations and the overall look will be in keeping with the style of Saxon and Norman decoration.

Tapestry colours

▶ Using paint colour charts from a DIY shop as examples, ask the children to select eight different colours from the tapestry and give each a name, for example Horseleg Green, Axe Red, Anchor Grey, Doublet Buff.

▶ The children could also try dyeing wool. Onion skins, fruit such as plums or blackberries, heather, lichen and chickweed all give colourful dye when boiled in water. The washed wool is then soaked for twenty-four hours in the liquid, wrung out and hung up to dry.

▶ On a piece of open-weave fabric, the children could practise stitches *à la* Bayeux Tapestry using the wool they have dyed.

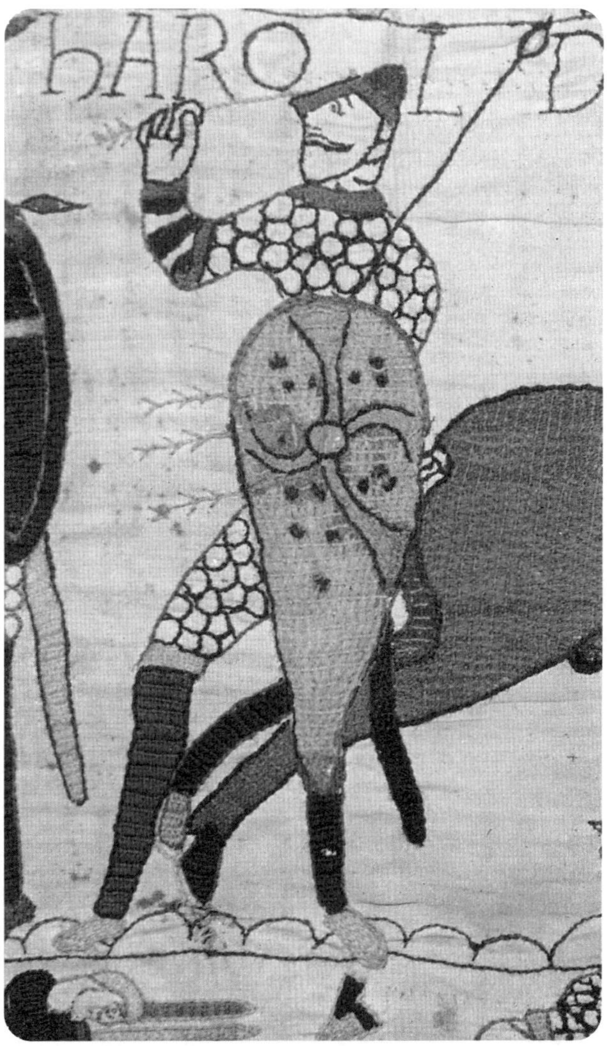

The Bayeux Tapestry

background information

The story behind the picture

1042 the Saxon, Edward the Confessor, became king. He died in 1066 and had no son or heir. There were two possible successors to the throne – Duke William of Normandy who was Edward's cousin, and Earl Harold of England who belonged to the most powerful family in England and was Edward's brother-in-law. Without waiting to find out the wishes of the people, Harold was crowned as king on the same day as the funeral without the consent of the bishops and nobles. The English were 'moved to anger' when they found out and things did not go well for him from the start. A comet appeared in the sky and was seen as a sign by the Saxons that trouble would ensue.

Across the Channel, incensed by Harold's audacity, Duke William started to organise an invasion. It took from January to August to build the boats and make the weapons. He had 5,000 foot-soldiers and 2,000 knights on horseback. The invasion took place, Norman Cavalry against Saxon Infantry. King Harold and his army were defeated near Hastings.

Saxon rule was over.

Picture facts

The original tapestry is 50 cm wide and 70.34 m long. The tapestry is really an embroidery worked in wool and features 626 people, 505 animals, 37 buildings and 41 ships. It was commissioned a decade after the battle by William's brother, Bishop Odo of Bayeux, to celebrate the victory. Although known as the Bayeux Tapestry, it is thought that nuns based in either Canterbury or Winchester embroidered it with the help, so legend says, of William's wife, Queen Matilda. It was displayed in Bayeux Cathedral on feast days and is mentioned on the church inventory in 1476.

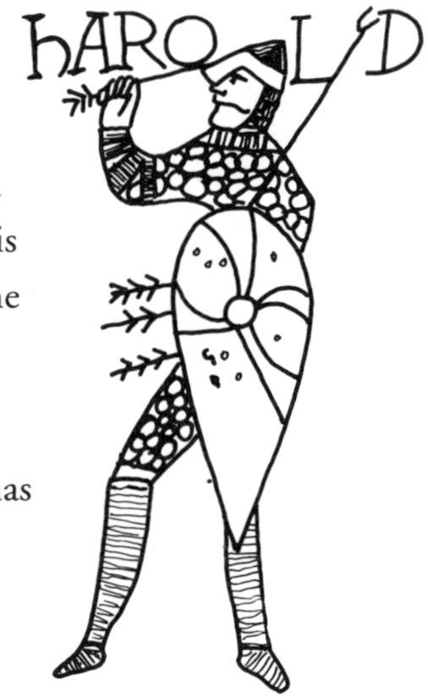

In 1842 it was taken to the library at Bayeux and, in 1873, photographed for the first time. It is now on display in the Palais de Justice in Bayeux, France.

Elizabeth and Thomas Wardle saw the embroidery in France in 1815 and after seeing photographs of the Bayeux Tapestry at the South Kensington Museum (now the Victoria and Albert Museum) developed the idea of a full-size replica 'so that England should have a copy of its own'.

The replica, now housed in the Museum of Reading, was sewn in 1886 by 35 Victorian ladies of the Leek Embroidery Society. It took just over a year to make. Like the original, it was sewn in two-ply wool yarn on linen and the original colours were carefully matched by Thomas Wardle by dyeing 100 pounds of yarn with natural dyes.

It was purchased for Reading Corporation in 1895 for £200 and shortly afterwards taken to Windsor for Queen Victoria to see. The replica was first shown in Leek, Staffordshire. Admission was one shilling and just over 1200 people saw it.

In 1886 it was exhibited in England, the United States and Germany. Finally, it was displayed in the new Art Gallery in Reading in 1897 where it was loaned for exhibitions until 1992. In 1927 the tapestry was taken down, cleaned, repaired and remounted as 25 separate panels, housed in dust-proof cases. It was restored again in 1993.

The Bayeux Tapestry comic strip

These pictures are miniature pictures from the Bayeux Tapestry.

▶ Write what you think is happening in each one underneath the picture.

1

2

3

4

PROGRAMME

5 Sir Henry Unton

Programme outline

The subject of this programme is a painting by an unknown artist about the life of Sir Henry Unton – a Tudor gentleman and ambassador. This picture is of particular interest to a class of children involved in a project about the Tudors and they set off for the National Portrait Gallery in search of further information about it.

Whilst seated on the floor studying a slide of the painting, the children are amazed to see Lady Dorothy Unton (who commissioned the painting) magically brought to life to talk about the picture. 'The right stages in the right order – is how to tell a story,' says Dorothy, responding to a query about where to begin and she tells the story of her 'marvellous brave' husband's life.

She describes her own duties as a Tudor lady. With her husband away a lot she was responsible for the running of the family home – Wadley Manor, near Oxford. Through chat and discussion, useful information about life in Tudor times is presented.

As well as commemorating her husband's life with a painting, Dorothy Unton commissioned John Dowland to write the music for a pavane, danced in celebration of her husband. Her last wish of the children is that they should dance this in memory of her husband.

Key features

- Historical enquiry
- Aspects of Tudor life
- Autobiographical narrative art

Before viewing

Discussion

▶ Talk with the class about the Tudor lifestyle and times. Tell the story of the painting (see page 22).

Assemble plenty of books – or better still visit a Tudor house so that children can see the style of life enjoyed by a person of Sir Henry's standing.

After viewing

About the picture

▶ Retell the story of Sir Henry Unton's life. Ask the children to tell it back to you in the manner of story consequences, with one child picking up the story when another leaves off.

Where are the darkest areas of the painting? Where are the lightest areas of the painting? Is there more dark than light? Why?

True or false

The children could work in pairs or groups to decide which of the statements on Activity sheet 5 are true or false and give the reasons why.

1. T	5. T	9. F
2. F	6. F	10. T
3. T	7. F	
4. F	8. T	

Sir Henry's travels

▶ What countries, cities or place names can the children point out on the painting (for example France, the Low Countries – The Netherlands, Padua, Venice, the Alps)?

▶ On a large wall map the class could see if these names have changed and plot Sir Henry Unton's travels.

▶ The journey from France to Oxfordshire took his coffin four days. How long do the children think such a journey would take today?

Interrogating the painting

▶ Ask the children to look closely at the picture and answer the following questions. It would help to use magnifying glasses.

- How many weeping servants can you count?
- Why is Sir Henry shown with his pen in the middle of the page, but he has written nothing?
- What was he going to write?
- Who are the gloomy people under the trees?
- Why is the picture so dark in colour?
- Why has Sir Henry such a bright, light face?
- Why are some people in the distance bigger than some people at the front?

The pavane

▶ Obviously home entertainment was different from that of today. Dancing and 'live' music were popular. Dancing took place inside large houses and barns, or else outside in the fresh air. The Resource sheet on page 28 gives the steps to the pavane: perhaps the children could dance this in memory of Sir Henry using John Dowland's specially commissioned music.

Children who enjoy playing the recorder could accompany the dancers (see page 28).

Tudor mini-portraits

▶ Each child takes a sheet of paper and folds it into eight. In each section they then sponge on eight flesh-coloured round blobs. When dry, they could draw features on the faces, for example beard, whiskers, hair, hat. Reference books will help to create convincing looking Tudor mini-portraits.

This is your life

▶ Ask the children to chart aspects of their lives from birth to the present. Their autobiographical details could cover many things from their family details, to where they live and the pets they have, to the name of their favourite activity or sport.

Designer jackets

▶ Using reference books the children could design incredibly splendid Tudor-style jackets for Sir Henry and Dorothy Unton to wear to a banquet.

Frozen tableaux

▶ A frozen tableaux is a way of capturing a 'snapshot' of time. Allocate one character to each child in the class using the list below. Either use the whole class together or split them into groups that echo different parts of Sir Henry Unton's life such as his childhood, his time at Oxford, in Italy, his wedding, his time in France, his illness and his funeral. Then, using their bodies, the children make a 'frozen' picture to represent a chosen moment in the story.

Characters

Lady Dorothy

The Nurse

Lady Dorothy's Maids (2)

Sir Henry's Oxford Tutor

Friends who went to Italy with him (several)

Vicar who married Sir Henry and Dorothy

Mandolin player

Flute player

Man at feast

Lady at feast

Servant/page in the Netherlands

Queen Elizabeth (who knighted him)

French King's Doctor

Girl with poultice

Apothecary (chemist)

Captain of ship

Woman who hired the horses

Inn Keeper

Inn Keeper's Wife

Men who carried coffin (several)

Mason who built Unton family tomb

Vicar who buried him

Sad workers on his land

Sir Henry Unton's Sister

Sir Henry Unton: A Tudor gentleman

background information

The story behind the picture

According to his wife, Sir Henry Unton was a good and honourable man and upon his death all who knew him were 'sorely grieved'. It is thought that Dorothy Unton commissioned the painting for personal reasons as a record of her husband's life. It was hung in the house for anyone visiting to see.

Sir Henry Unton was born around 1557 at Wynchwood House in Oxfordshire. His grandfather had been knighted at Ann Boleyn's wedding.

The order of the picture, starting in the bottom right-hand corner, is as follows:

His birth, family crest, nursery scene including wet nurses and swaddling clothes. (Note the carpet – the Unton's were the 4th family in the country to possess one.)

When he was 16, he went to Oxford University, probably Oriel College, to study. See him at the window. Then he travelled to Venice to complete his studies.

He returned home proudly armed with what is reputed to be an Italian invention, the umbrella. Dorothy married the fine young man and the good times began. Song, dance, fun and lovely feasts. A splendid Tudor house, but sadly no children.

Sir Henry went on long journeys – first to fight for the Queen in the Netherlands (that's where he earned his knighthood), then to France as ambassador where he caught a 'mortal' fever and died. Although he was given the best possible treatment – using poultices and leeches to let blood – even the King of France's own doctor couldn't save him.

Much is made of the man. After his death in France around 1596 he was brought back across the channel in a black sailing ship and his coffin was pulled by black-draped horses all the way to the funeral in the church at Faringdon, Oxfordshire. After his funeral, he was placed in the family tomb where his wife later joined him.

Picture facts

This is a deep, dark, picture that meanders rather curiously through Sir Henry Unton's life. Richly painted in oils, it has little perspective and presents a series of symbolic cameos full of meaning; for example the sun presiding over the right of the painting symbolises light and peace whilst the moon on the left represents darkness and sorrow. Sir Henry himself is always portrayed larger than anyone else.

Many aspects of wealthy Tudor lifestyle are represented in the painting:

- The bare-headed musicians are not Sir Henry's gentlemen friends but paid musicians.
- Because people ate with their fingers, napkins were worn on the collar or sleeve, and used to wipe dirty fingers on.
- Many poor people came to watch the funeral.
- There are two chests either side of the tomb. Like the Canopic jars in Ancient Egypt, the one on the left contains the 'soft bits' and on the right the 'hard bits' from the embalming process.

The artist who painted it is not known, neither is the length of time it took to paint. The painting measures 163.2 cm wide and 74 cm high and is currently exhibited at the National Portrait Gallery and about one million visitors are recorded each year.

True or false?

Here is a list of statements about Sir Henry Unton's painting.

▶ Put a tick against each one in either the TRUE or FALSE column.

	TRUE	FALSE
1. The spooky sign that tells us Sir Henry is dead is a skeleton.		
2. Sir Henry died in Italy.		
3. At meal-times Tudor people did not eat with proper knives and forks.		
4. In Tudor times all men wore hats.		
5. Dorothy Unton was Sir Henry Unton's wife.		
6. Dorothy Unton painted this picture herself.		
7. Oxford is in the Netherlands.		
8. A pavane is a slow and careful dance.		
9. Sir Henry's favourite food was French fries.		
10. Sir Henry died in 1596.		

▶ With a partner make up five more TRUE or FALSE statements.

PROGRAMME 6

The Railway Station by William Frith

Programme outline

Paddington Station provides the setting for the opening of this programme. Here a class of children are making a contemporary representation of the station through sketches, photographs and video as part of their work on the Victorians. To get a sense of how the same station would have looked in Victorian days, they also visit an art gallery to view a painting of it which was completed by William Frith in 1863. They try to imagine what it would be like to be the people in the picture.

One class member is transported back in time to Frith's studio where he is eagerly awaited by the artist. As Frith's model for the day, the boy poses as one of the central characters in the painting and engages in a dialogue with the painter which serves to convey useful (and sometimes amusing) information about Mr Frith, his way of working and life at the time.

Train design evolved from the horse-drawn carriages. Mr Frith explains that at first, poor people would travel in open rail trucks and the wealthy in closed compartments. The design of these were changed, so that everyone travelled in enclosed carriages with their luggage on the roof.

Mr Frith is horrified when his model produces some of the photographs that were taken by the class. He can't believe the way railway engines have changed and horror of horrors – women are wearing trousers!

Key features

- Rail travel
- Representations of and attitudes to Victorian life
- Public life and leisure

Before viewing

▶ Talk with the class about their experiences of rail travel. Find out what they know generally about stations; for example who runs them and when they were built.

▶ Introduce the idea that in the Victorian period, train travel was hugely popular and prepare the class for the programme by telling them the story behind the painting of 'The Railway Station' (see page 26).

Whilst viewing

▶ Ask the children to look at the way modern images are contrasted with Victorian images throughout the programme. How observant are they? Can they spot the surprise visitor to Paddington station at the end of the programme (it's Paddington Bear!).

After viewing

About the picture

▶ What did the children think about Mr Frith painting things in to the picture that were not really there just to please prospective buyers?

▶ If the painting had been wider in width what other images would the children continue the picture with? Perhaps there would be more of the scene around the criminal being arrested.

- How many people are in the painting? How many men, women, children, animals?
- What sort of clothes are people wearing?
- What sort of things are happening in the picture?
- Where are the darkest areas of the painting? Where are the lightest areas of the painting? Is there more dark than light? Why?

Colour matching

▶ Children will need to work in pairs on this task of looking at colour and texture within the painting. First they fold a large piece of paper into eight. From a selection of fabric samples, they then match different pieces of material to the colours in the painting, stick them down and note beneath each one who in the painting was wearing that colour, e.g. bridesmaid
silky yellow dress.

Character traits

▶ Working together in a small group, the children could look up the definitions in a dictionary and then find people in the painting to fit the following descriptions:

happy

sad

grumpy

worried

healthy

friendly

ill

unkind

sulky

vague

arrogant

deceitful

trustworthy

▶ They could then make up a name and occupation for their chosen characters, for example: Sara the sulky seamstress, George the worried ship owner.

People and postcards

▶ Give out Activity sheet 6 and ask the children to work on it either individually or in pairs.

An extension of this activity would be for the children to make a card for someone in the painting to send to another person in the painting, for example soldier to wife, detective to brother. The picture could be of the place they have gone to or a comic scene or even a postcard copy of the railway station painting.

The task is to write something interesting rather than 'arrived safely'. They could also invent an address and draw a Victorian stamp.

Conversation piece

▶ The children could work in fours to re-create the conversations occurring between four people in the picture.

Rules: start with a frozen tableau. The conversation must last for two minutes only. It finishes in a new freeze.

Station sounds

▶ Stations are noisy places. In groups, children could role-play the imagined conversations of some of the people in the painting. Others can imitate a variety of different sounds, for example engines, whistles, pigeons, footsteps, dogs.

▶ Rather than tape record a cacophony of uncontrolled sound, have a class conductor who selects the group or groups who do their sound effects, thereby compiling an interesting sound effect to accompany the picture.

Effects could overlap and the Railway Station tape, when completed, could be hidden near the picture to surprise unsuspecting visitors!

The Railway Station by William Frith

background information

The story behind the picture

The painting was commissioned by Mr Flatow who was an agent and knew that the painting would sell because art was very popular in Victorian times. The growth of the middle classes provided a new market for art. As potential buyers, the Victorians and their moral values often determined the content of paintings. Flatow himself wanted to be in the picture and he can be seen talking to the engine driver.

Frith knew that his customers liked 'nice, cosy scenes' hanging on their walls. One reason for including the scene (to the right of the painting) of two policemen issuing a warrant for arrest, was because of the Victorian concern about criminality. However, he was sensible enough to balance this with concepts of 'gainful employment', fragile beauty and a fashionable wedding party in crinoline dresses.

In his diary, Frith offered sound advice to his pupils; 'I desire to reiterate for the information of young painters that every object, living or dead was painted from nature.'

Frith very much wanted the painting to sell, so he angled the scene towards an exaltation of Victorian middle and upper class prosperity. Such wealthy folk are central to the picture and there is little evidence of the pain and poverty of Victorian times. Even the rubbish and the litter is depicted prettily, although the railways employed a huge workforce to clean and there was not so much packaging as today anyway. Interestingly, the walls of the station were covered in advertising hoardings but Frith chose to cover these in the picture with a romantic image of the train.

Picture facts

Platforms, porters, policemen, people coming and going, steam and the hustle and bustle of stations. Expectations tinged with fears, joys and disappointments. No wonder Frith chose this subject for his painting – and little wonder it was successful.

Frith visited the station regularly in order to collect ideas and information via his chalk drawings, but he also used photographs and tableaux of people in his studio and his own family as models for the group – for example the foreign visitor being cheated by the taxi driver was his daughter's Italian teacher and the family in the middle was Frith's own, sending their son away to school.

'The Railway Station' was painted in oil in 1863. It was purchased in 1869. The whole process of creating and executing the painting took about two years.

In seven weeks, 21,550 people queued and paid to see the painting. People fainted with excitement! Thousands of engravings were made and sold (today's equivalent of buying videos). Later, five copies of the painting were produced in oils.

Victorian postcards

The world's first postcards were issued on 1st October 1869 in Australia.

To begin with they did not have pictures and the idea of them was to extend the business of the post office by encouraging people to write to each other.

In 1870, about the time of 'The Railway Station' painting by William Frith, people in Britain began to send postcards. By 1st October 1870, half a million had been sent. In 1900, 500 million cards were sent. (Remember that there were no telephones or radios in 1900.)

▶ This is an example of a Victorian postcard.

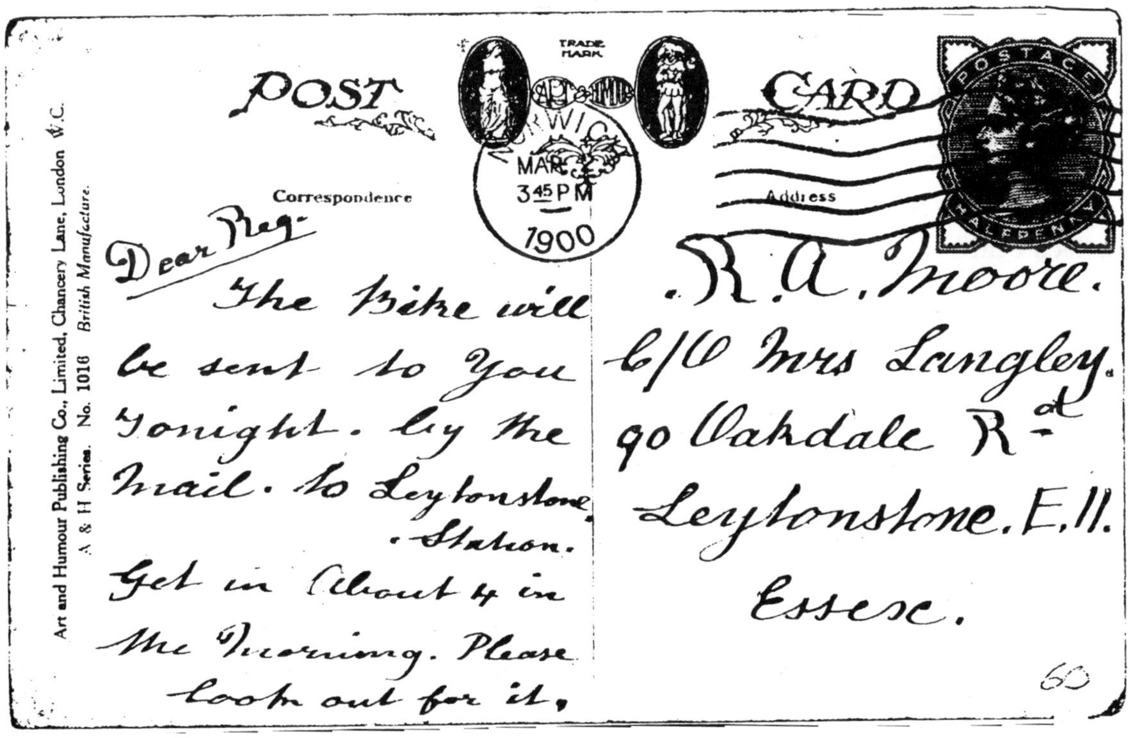

▶ Can you answer these questions?

- Who sent this card?
- What year did they post it?
- Who is the queen on it?
- What do you think the house it was delivered to looked like?
- Who was it sent to?
- How much did the stamp cost?
- Who do you think received it?

The pavane (Programme 5 – Sir Henry Unton)

Pavane – a grave and stately processional dance in which the dancers are elaborately dressed. It was introduced into England in the sixteenth century. The music for the dance has a very slow rhythm.

Steps to the pavane

The music requires slow, dignified movements with the head held high.
The dancers hold hands in pairs in two lines facing forwards.

Walking forwards

1. Reverence – a bow and a curtsey
2. Step to the left (1 beat) – left foot follows (1 beat); eyes look left
3. Step to the right (1 beat) – right foot follows (1 beat); eyes look right
4. Walk forward on left foot for one step (1 beat)
5. Walk forward on right foot for one step (1 beat)
6. Walk forward on left foot for one step (1 beat)
7. Feet together, return to starting position
8. Step to the right (1 beat) – left foot follows (1 beat); eyes look right
9. Step to the left (1 beat) – right foot follows (1 beat); eyes look left

Walking backwards

10. Step backwards on right foot for one step, then left foot, then right foot and feet together; nod facing each other
11. Follow steps 2-3

Change direction

To face opposite end of room – partner on right walks round partner on left in anti-clockwise direction. Repeat as necessary.

John Dowland's music